Platinum Publishing

Shirin Ariff Sabir

THE SECOND
Wife

Seduced Into Slavery

Platinum Publishing
c/o Fatima Omar Khamissa
18-3555 Don Mills Road
Suite 131
Toronto
Ontario
M2H 3N3

Like anything in life, there are no guarantees that using the methods mentioned by the publisher of by any of the contributors will result in the same success mentioned.

Although the author and publisher have made every effort to ensure that the information in this book was correct at press time, the author and publisher do not assume and hereby disclaim any liability to any party for any loss, damage, or disruption caused by errors or omissions, whether such errors or omissions result from negligence, accident, or any other cause.

The information contained within this book is strictly for educational purposes. If you wish to apply ideas contained in this book, you are taking full responsibility for your actions

Typesetting and formatting by access.ideas@yahoo.com

ISBN: 978-0-9953136-5-1

Platinum Publishing

ACKNOWLEDGEMENT

I am grateful for every single moment that I have experienced in my life and even for the moments to come. I am grateful for the awareness that at any given time, *this* is my time.

I am humbled by the contributions made by every human being I crossed paths with, as family, relatives, friends, neighbours, co-workers and my teachers, mentors and coaches.

I would never dare say that I am self-made. I am the result of the sum of interactions and experiences I have had with all the people I met in my life and my willingness to learn from them. Gosh, there are so many of you to appreciate and I see this as a privilege. In counting you, I feel blessed.

I *agree* to be free

The Second Wife

The last leaf has fallen
It lies in dust
What is love today?
Convenience and lust
Recycle, use, and throw
Is the talk of the town!
No one really cares
If you smile or frown
The dreams I dreamt of love
Those dreams were only mine
I am now but a broken heart
There's grief in every whine
You broke the law of Nature
We are only made in twos
You chose me to be punished
While deceit pulled you through
Our futures are destined
I've been a married lonesome heart
May the sins of your betrayal
Always, always keep us apart

CONTENTS

PROLOGUE

As an immigrant woman living in Canada, I have learned that many women have experienced trauma in their birth countries, especially countries outside the western world. Traumas such as rape, dowry deaths, female infanticide, and child marriages are very common. When we migrate to the western world, it then takes us a while to realize what exists for us as women here.

I went through mental, emotional, and financial abuse for quite a few years, justifying to myself that *at least* there was no physical abuse. *At least* can sometimes be such a disempowering narrative in our minds. It is like saying a*t least* I had rotten food to eat instead of having no food to eat. This state of compromise comes from a loss of self-worth and dignity, from not being able to identify any kind of abuse as abuse.

Until I woke up to recognise the abuse, I was stuck and kept choosing it in my life. I had to regain the power of being my own stand, the power of saying enough is enough; the power of saying *no*, the power of choosing me.

Until I had my own painful experiences, I was

oblivious of the various types of abuse. My pain gave me compassion not only for others like the *Rohingya* victims, where the abuse is extreme and cannot go unnoticed but for those who carry several unseen scars of mental and emotional abuse hiding behind the facade of a so called progressive world. It shows up in the clever guise of unequal pay for women or deprivation from higher paid positions. In my own experiences, I know now that that is also an abuse.

On inquiring further, I learnt that there are six broader categories of abuse, namely, physical, verbal or emotional, financial, mental, sexual and cultural. Despite several intervention programs to prevent domestic violence, abuse seems to be an epidemic that plagues our entire world. What was heart-breaking was the shattering of my belief, that the western countries were abuse free territories.

I am writing this book in retrospect. Today, I am the same person and yet, I am not who I was choosing to be in the earlier chapters of the book of my life. Before I begin my story, I want you to know this: *I am Okay*. That I changed the narrative of my life and it is possible. I made it. I chose not to return to India like *Chand*, played by Indian actor Preity Zinta in the Bollywood film, *Heaven on Earth* by Deepa Mehta in 2008.

In the film, Chand is a Punjabi woman from India, who marries an Indo-Canadian man from our very own Brampton in Ontario. She immigrates to Canada and ends up in an abusive marriage to eventually succumb under the pressure of abuse. She chooses separation and returns to India. This may be the story of a few immigrant women who came here with dreams of a beautiful future. I personally know of one who secretly pleaded for money from her neighbours and friends to afford her escape by flight to India and another who was beaten up by her husband and locked up in her closet, right here in Canada. Why have these stories not caught the attention of the stakeholders in our Canadian community? Why do people not hear the voices of such diminished women? I found the answer with Statistics Canada. Out of every 1000 women who are sexually abused, only 33 are reported to the police! This ratio has remained almost the same from 2004 to 2014.

On further research I discovered that the National Domestic Violence Hotline of USA used the Duluth Model of Power and Control Wheel to detail about Relationship Violence. According to the model, the various kinds of abusive behaviour are:

- Coercion and threats
- Intimidation
- Emotional abuse
- Isolation
- Minimizing, denying and blaming

- Using children
- Economic abuse
- Male privilege

(Source: https://www.thehotline.org/2013/08/20/taking-a-spin-around-the-power-and-control-wheel/)

The most interesting part is that all these behaviours are often disguised as everyday relationship dynamics in many homes. I have personally experienced some of these behaviours without ever seeing them as abuse. What may be considered as abuse may perhaps be the normal narrative in many homes. In fact a lot of these behaviours are used to raise well-disciplined children. These children then grow up to never see themselves being abused because to them it is the way they were raised.

Despite the hush about violence behind closed doors of Canadian homes, in reference to South Asian families particularly, Stats Canada has tabulated the following ridiculously unbelievable scenario for South Asian women and their relationship status in 2009. How far have we progressed in 10 years?

Violence faced by South Asian Women:

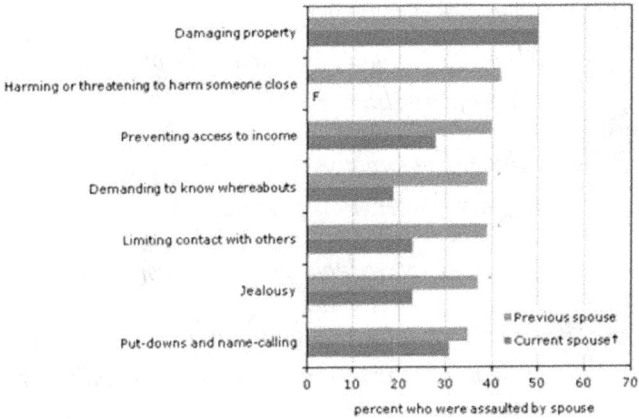

percent who were assaulted by spouse

(Source: https://www150.statcan.gc.ca/n1/pub/85-002-x/2013001/article/11766/11766-2-eng.htm)

Let us make this book alive and interactive so that it can serve as intended.

Exercise:

- *My request would be for you to be present to the following words:*

- *Abuse, Compromise, Adjust, Compassion, Dignity, Power, Possibility, and Self-worth.*

- *Sometimes we assume what these words mean.*

- *Be present to the emotions and/or experiences that these words stir in you as you say them and write them down. Once you have written them down, I invite you to then look up the meanings of these words in a dictionary. Discover for yourself if the meanings you are making of them are different from what they actually mean?*

Notes:

THE PRESENT

I am not writing this book in literary pursuit. In your generous listening, I am encouraged to tell my story of heart-breaks, failures and victory and be heard.

I am sharing my tears of trauma and my cries of triumph with you. I am writing to you with the urgency to make a difference. I was buried for years. I was lost in the depths of my own fears and diminution to discover that silence is a facilitator of abuse. Now, I have found myself again and have learned to trust my inner wisdom. It will never fail me. If you are ever lost, there is a way back. I have discovered a portal of return to self, a path to resurgence.

Yes, I broke free and reached an almost super heroic state of manifestation. A far cry from feeling trapped in my own insecurities and low self-worth. I didn't even have to do as much as snap my fingers to call a genie. I became my own genie and my own true love.

My world, my life, along with those of my children's, has taken a full turn for the best so far. After over a decade of suffering in Canada, we are happy, at peace, and living a life that is very fulfilling.

I cut the cord of abuse. I aborted the legacy of abuse from permeating the lives of my children, in the name of culture.

Abuse is not my culture.

I have recently returned from a vacation. We visited places I had read of as a child and dreamed of the day I would visit them. London seemed like we were playing inside the game of Monopoly; Morocco was perhaps from the pages of Aladdin and the Magic Lamp!

We travelled across three continents and the experience was beyond my imagination. We saw places that were not on my list. The Universe was in giving mode, and I had no desire to stop receiving. The whole world was ours. We had learned to own it. We visited the Buckingham Palace in London and the Chateau de Versailles in France. We saw the Montjuic in Barcelona, and the Alhambra Palace in Andalucía. We visited the Rock of Gibraltar, in Gibraltar and the Sintra Palacio in Lisbon. We deserved this experience for we had learned to embrace the whole world as our own.

On another trip, I visited Haiti. In a complete contrast to the grandeur of the palaces we saw in Europe, their simple living was very attractive. They had nothing, and yet, they were joyful and content, with whatever little they had. Perhaps some of the kings and queens of those palaces yearned for this freedom. It was a world within a world that was free of internet and technology. The people had no cell phones, computers, or televisions. The children had hand-crafted toys and created their own from wood. The place was lush and beautiful. We witnessed a healing chapter; a voodoo dance by the village head. My son felt special as he was picked by the healer to participate in the healing ceremony. My children were also intrigued to watch sugarcane juice made from crushing sugarcane sticks by twisting them by hand. They had never seen or tasted anything like that before.

I seemed to be revisiting my childhood days. I loved chilled sugarcane juice from street vendors on a sweltering after school day. I would watch them crush the juice out of these long sticks of sweetness by using a mill. It took two men to do this. One of them hand spun the mill while the other fed the sugarcane sticks to the mill over and over again until they looked like straw. "No ginger for me please", I would say. My taste for ginger was acquired after I came to live in this western world and couldn't take its presence for granted anymore. I began to miss the aroma of this spice that is gaining popularity here. I preferred the lemon and lots of ice. Not only did I stand in the sun and drink them from earthen pots, we filled our water bottles to take them home for another round of that drink. This felt like abundance. As kids, we found joy in little things.

I did not have a cell phone or a computer or the internet not because we could not afford them but because they did not exist as commodities in every home in India. We played like we were born free with not a worry in the world. There was a thrill in playing hide-and-seek or in making our own toys. From paper boats to sophisticated paper folded airplanes, we took pride in our creations. Team play was so compelling. There is no greater joy than playing with real people, brainstorming together, learning to be mindful of others, forgiving and seeking forgiveness, being in allowance and problem solving, caring for each other. The controlling world of virtual play and simulation that gives the experience of absolute control to a child can never replace these real life experiences. It gave us the opportunity to grow and get along with others, there was no other way. We could not have wasted our childhood in isolation; we had to learn the art of getting along. That is the key to successful relationships not only with others but with your own self first.

We couldn't wait to start the games. We got to learn to make our own kites and fly them! What a sense of victory that was! We learnt to give, to share, our precious marbles. Some of them were favourites and too hard to part with. We crushed leaves and flowers and used peels to pretend to cook up a meal or dipped our hands in dye while exploring with the art of tie and dye. We saw how cows were milked and guarded eggs for the hens in our coops. Crows had to back off. I knew how to use a catapult! We prattled with parrots and danced with fan tailed pigeons. We waded our way home in knee deep waters of Indian monsoons and waited to see caterpillars turn into butterflies. I was more scared to see a gecko than the gecko that had lost its tail in escaping the danger it saw in me! From pet dogs, cats, goats, ducks, parrots, squirrels, turkey, a monkey and a pet ram, we grew up experiencing compassion for animals, right in our own homes. My imagination was limitless and a pet baby elephant was definitely next on my wish list!

Our trip to Morocco seemed like we were time travelling. It reconnected me with the fresh and home-made food that I grew up eating. My grandmother's kitchen was where abundance was served every day. It had food for everyone, very delicious food that was cooked meticulously from scratch. The process was elaborate and demanded commitment. The hotel we stayed in was actually a mansion. The women in the family ran the kitchen. Yogurt and freshly squeezed fruit juice were made daily. Homemade jellies, warm from the oven pita bread, and aromatic Moroccan Mint tea set the tone for the day. I could have lived here forever. I was tempted to imagine that *Bela* and *Gulshan*, my grandmother's cooks would just run out of that kitchen to hug me! They were no less than family. I feel pain in my heart that I will never see them again.

Argan oil churners, snake charmers, and belly dancers filled the markets. The souks and donkey carts in the narrow alleys reminded me of Tintin Stories. I would walk home from school, down a similar alley near my home. At every nook I had a cousin or a cousin's friend idling their time on the streets, dressed like Bollywood heroes, sitting on their shiny motorcycles. I was always safe and protected. On the other hand I could never get to do anything sneaky without being caught and reported to my parents!

Exotic spices, strong fragrances, and rich rugs brought back my childhood dreams. Life was simpler back then. There was more time to read books, plant a seed and wait for a flower to blossom. More time to count stars, find shapes in puffy clouds, to watch the rain for hours, make paper boats, count colours in a rainbow and daydream of flying on magic carpets. I was the princess of my dreams!

Exercise:

- *What do you dream of?*
- *My vision board is a display of my wishes on my refrigerator door.*
- *There are pictures from magazines, cut and put on the refrigerator door! A few fridge magnets hold them in place.*
  - *Where are you planning your next vacation to be?*
  - *How would your future home look like?*
  - *Are you wishing for a life partner or a dream job?*
- *Dream, dream, dream away*
- *Be excited about it. Flip through magazines and catalogues to find the pictures that are close to the ones in your dreams.*
- *The pictures that light you up, the pictures that tug at your heart!*
- *Find them, keep them.*
- *Have them around you where you can see them and connect with them. Make your dreams a part of your daily lives. Make them a part of your present for them to show up for real in your lives.*
- *Be a co-creator of your own life.*
- *Be your own Genie!*

Notes: ✍

My Roots

I come from a very prestigious family of Kolkata, India. My lineage includes royalty. I am related to the granddaughter of Tipu Sultan's family. He was the king of Mysore, India. My ancestors were also flourishing silk merchants and industrialists who came to India from Samarkand and Bukhara. They were the proud owners of the first silk mill in West Bengal, India. We were the *Zamindars* or landlords of British India.

The other day, I met the host of an Indian restaurant in Toronto who mentioned he lived on *Ariff* Road, Calcutta, and I smiled. That is what my ancestors had achieved. Even though I have been shy about sharing these details with the people around me, I am proud to say that my ancestors were "giants" in the community. They left enormous footprints for us. Unfortunately, it has been hard to fit in those shoes. In February of 2017, the beautiful palatial home, the last remnants of our glory, the house that I was born in, burned in a big fire and was lost forever.

Growing up in a large family was joyful as well as confronting. I grew up in a world of dualities. At times, we were a loving, united family, but we also fought and had grievances over property matters. There was a huge list of what we as girls could never do. It was not easy being a girl. It was not easy being controlled by a dozen elders giving you conflicting orders. I was always confused with so many different perspectives and often couldn't take a stand on any.

I had over twenty cousins in the extended family to share my childhood with. We all lived in the same house. As for my own siblings, I have a sister and a brother. I am the oldest amongst them. My favourite moments were when all of us played. And the times we spent together during festivals and weddings. As a child, I was timid, gullible, and sometimes bullied.

I was also curious and engaged in learning. The elders in the family taught me sewing, knitting, painting, cooking, and craft work. I learned them as part of my everyday life. There was exposure to different cultures and food traditions. I learned to speak, read, and write several languages. English, Bengali, Hindi, Urdu, and bragged of knowing a few words in Hakka Chinese too! The biggest gift that my family gave to me was the ability to embrace diversity. Muslims, Hindus, Chinese, and Jewish communities were part of my family. I acquired the ability to assimilate with people anywhere without feeling uncomfortable. My happiest memories are those of my school days and play time at home with all my siblings and peers.

Property disputes tore up the beautiful and rich fabric of our family. This left me sad and heartbroken. The women had no say and at times it got really obnoxious when they screamed and argued. They had to support the men in their family.

As a child, I witnessed the ugly conflicts that involved shouting matches, verbal violation, aggravation, and physical assault amongst my elders. I grew up fearing them instead of loving and trusting them. Unfortunately, one relationship that demanded endurance was my father's second cousin, Aleph. Aleph is Sahir's brother, Maira's husband. Sahir and I ended up marrying each other later in life.

Aleph did not want my father to be trustee of the family estate. He expressed the desire to be trustee by virtue of seniority. Unfortunately, he was also an alcoholic, lovely otherwise. I have fond memories of him asking me to choose which horse he should bet on. Yes, he would bet on race-horses everyday! He was very respectful with children though and best friends with my loving uncle Nasir.

Papa would always say that Aleph was a thorough gentleman. Papa blamed his violent and abusive behaviour on his chronic addiction to alcohol. And the desperate need for money to support the "Nawab" lifestyle of betting and alcoholism. I wish he was alive and I could share with him what Sahir did to me. He visits me in my dreams and comforts me. He would not be happy.

Exercise:

- *Aleph was often judged for his addiction.*

- *Is there anyone in your family that you haven't met or spoken with in a long time?*

- *Is there anyone in your family who left you feeling unheard and incomplete?*

- *Is there anyone in your family who is heavily judged?*

- *I invite you to call someone you haven't spoken with in a long time. Reach out to them and share with them all those unsaid thoughts.*

- *Seek completion in a conversation if you have a grievance: Share with them what you have been feeling and invite them to share with you what they have been feeling. This can restore and renew your relationship with them.*

- *Unsaid words and incomplete experiences take up a lot of space in your minds.*

- *Clear the clutter in your mind. Be free.*

Notes:

Uncle in Love

"Don't call me uncle," he said.
"What do I call you?"
"Call me Sahir," he replied.

It is a common tradition in India for people to show respect to those older than them- we do not call our elders by name. Particularly, respectful women in traditional families like ours had a protocol. Based on how young or old they looked we were expected to safely define a man who is not family, as *brother* or *uncle*. This was done to set healthy boundaries and expectations. In our times of growing up in India, in some families, the idea of girls having male friends was not considered morally correct. If a girl spoke to a boy, it led to terrible gossip. Gossip aimed at morally condemning the girl, and the family feared that it would be hard to get her married.

Sahir is Aleph's brother-in-law, the same Uncle Aleph I mentioned in my last chapter. My cousin, Gizel, called him *Mamu*, which means maternal uncle in the Indian language. Gizel is older than me. So it was assumed that he was *Mamu* to us siblings and peers even though he was not *my* mother's brother.

Sahir said later that he had silently nurtured love for me since the day he had first seen me as a teen girl. He watched me while I played with my siblings. I was rarely allowed to go downstairs. His sister lived there with her family and other relatives. I may have been around 16 years old then, he said. And since then, his eyes would yearn to get a glimpse of me. He claimed to have waited for 25 long years for this moment of reconnection. By a turn of fate, his silent wish of having an encounter with me became fulfilled. We reconnected after my first marriage fell apart.

Notes: ✍

_____

_____

_____

_____

_____

_____

_____

_____

_____

_____

_____

_____

_____

_____

_____

_____

My First Marriage

In 2000, I had ended my first marriage of eight years. I was devastated. In the Chutes and Ladders of the game of life, I was back to square one – my parents' home. It had been eight years of loving and nurturing gone waste. We did not hate each other. The divorce was to stop further damage. I was only 22 when I married Junaid. I was very young and in the last year of my undergraduate studies.

A lot of sincere hard work went into dealing with adversity that arose from trying to keep my family together. I am grateful to a few generous relatives who chose to be greater human beings and attempted to save our marriage. The best that happened from that marriage was my beautiful daughter, Sabah, who lives with me. I can't imagine what my life would have been without her contributions of grace and wisdom to my family. She was 6 years old when I went back to my parents. The experience had an impact on her little mind. At her tender age, what she saw was that I had left her father whom she loved dearly, and she had no idea why I did that. She is a beautiful young lady now and she understands. She is my best friend, secret keeper, my voice of wisdom, and my life-saver - Sabah. Despite all my misfortunes, her presence in my life makes me the most fortunate woman on this planet. Sabah is a gift, and you will see that as the story of my life unfolds. Sabah has been my partner in knowing emotional and financial hardship from a very young age. A drug-addict's daughter, she has experienced struggle, rejection and anxiety from childhood.

We had not shared with the extended family that Junaid, my first husband, was a drug addict. Some of the people around me were quick to judge that it must have been my fault. Their creativity was at its peak when conjecturing my divorce. They fabricated stories and accused me of having an extra-marital affair. They even accused little Sabah to have brought bad luck to us, her parents. I was in the limelight of our family buzz. Thank God gossip does not spark a wildfire, or the whole world could be destroyed by it. Nevertheless, it hurt us. We were made to be wrong and to feel humiliated. At a time when it was so hard for us to give up on our family and our home, no one was thinking about what it was like to be us– heartbroken, ashamed, extremely stressed and hurt. I had no clue of what my future looked like. The present was a challenge to endure.

In our lives in India, during those days when I was dealing with my divorce, there was no such thing as *depression* for us because there was not much awareness about it. We had to deal with whatever challenges came our way. We embraced life with all its ups and downs. It was expected of us to go through whatever we had to go through and bounce back to life on our own. We did not know any other way. This was a blessing in disguise because it taught us to be brave and take charge of our lives. The need for counselling and medication did not exist. It was a belief that only people with serious mental disorders sought counselling. There was not a lot of family support. In response to the crisis in my life, I would sleep a lot to escape facing it. My body went into sleep mode most of the time to escape my feelings of anxiety and stress. I had to process my grief. Not everyone in my family understood that and didn't show compassion. The gift in that was that I had to show up in my life and deal with my grief. I became a responsible adult and single mother as a result of this tough love.

My first husband, Junaid's addiction has a story that gives context to his choices. He had lost his mother to the hands of death by a fire accident. He was a very young child then and he never overcame the trauma of seeing his mother burnt alive. That experience dominated all the choices he made in his life. One of them being the use and abuse of substance- from smoking and sniffing drugs to injecting them, he did them all.

My experiences of living with him opened up a whole new world. It was a world of excuses, guilt, blame and shame; A world of peddlers, needles, heroin, pills, alcohol and borrowing money. Things went missing from home. Narcotics Anonymous meetings, counselling, drug rehab centres, and pawn shops became part of my daily routine. A whole new list of experiences that I had never seen or heard before became a part of my daily life. In fact, I did not know that drug addiction existed in India. I grew up very sheltered and protected with no idea of how things were outside of my realm of knowing.

We did everything we could to save our marriage. We relocated to different cities and attempted to make several fresh starts. We also moved into my parents' home for a while. Thereafter, we lived in the homes of generous relatives who eventually got fed up of trying in vain. We depleted every resource and were homeless and penniless. Our last stop when our family was still together was at my father-in-law's house. He had a challenging time believing and putting up with his son's addiction. Being a teetotaller, it was very hard for him to accept and understand the addiction of his only son. Besides, he was torn between his commitments towards his other wife and her two children. The wife who had taken charge of his home after Junaid's mother had died. He conditioned himself to believe that his son's addiction was my fault. How could I not change him and make him give up on drugs with my tender loving? I was not a rehabilitation expert, I was his wife. Of course, I did not know how to wean him away from narcotics.

I was living a tough lesson in forgiveness. Junaid was calm, well mannered, and brilliant. He was very well-read and intelligent. We shared the taste of good literature and music. He was a skilled computer programmer and wrote poetry like the muse. There were so many gifts he had for us to appreciate him for, and yet, he found comfort in drugs.

The stress of living eight years with a drug addict had its impact on me. I experienced a steep decline in my ability to trust people. I was always stressed and quick to react and be defensive. I learned to become suspicious. Even though he was not vicious, his addiction compelled him to lie. By the end of our marriage, I was sick with suspicion and worry. I lived moment to moment in fear of getting the news that he had died of an overdose or was arrested. The latter was perceived as shameful and embarrassing. I grew up in a home that never had to deal with any of this. Often I would cover up for Junaid.

After the divorce, I was left with a load of financial loans, the pain and shame of being an addict's wife, a miscarriage, and the responsibility of raising my child. It caused me immense stress. I had to maintain a healthy relationship between Junaid and our child. I had to pay the bills. One by one, we had exhausted our family support system. I was very young then and my life now has meandered its way into my forties. I realize that had I known then what I know now, perhaps I would have made different choices in my life. I have also learned that drug addicts will remain one for as long as *they choose to*. Only *they* could choose to be in the addiction or to quit the addiction. And only *they* had the right to define themselves as one for as long as *they* chose to.

Today, we share a daughter between us and live our own lives, miles apart, far away from each other. We continue to respect each other. I have no regrets about my experience of being his wife. I am grateful for my daughter. She carries the same spark of brilliance as her father. The experiences that came with this marriage taught me lessons in acceptance. It was also a very tough lesson on the experience of letting go and on the practice of unconditional love.

Exercise:

- *Last year, I completed a Canadian course as a Mental Health First Aid Provider. It equipped me with a better knowing and understanding of mental health.*

- *I recognised that there are so many people who are silently suffering. Sometimes they are misunderstood and ridiculed for their mental health conditions.*

- *I encourage you to volunteer at a mental health institute or an addiction rehab for a few days. Share your discovery with at least two people in your family who have no idea about mental health.*

- *This action will make a significant contribution to global inclusiveness and compassion.*

- *We change the world one person at a time.*

- *As divorce-rates increase, so do suicide, anxiety, abuse, stress and gun-violence. Education and understanding is needed. We need to see these not merely as terms, but as reality that human beings are dealing with as a result of complications in life.*

- *The breakdown comes from the pressure of handling challenging circumstances.*

Notes: ✍

Second Marriage

I was living at my parents' house, divorced, and as it occurred to me then, doomed. I found solace and spent most of my time at home in prayers. Praying gave me peace. My only inspiration was my daughter, Sabah.

Life was not the same for us. My mother was angry and frustrated. My father was helpless and grieving with me. The habitual gossip of some of my relatives and my child's silent suffering bothered me. There was a lot I had to deal with, not excluding my own inner dialogue of failure and personal worth. I was weighed down from dealing with other peoples' emotions and disappointments. I had no time to address my own feelings. I would repress them.

What was it like for me to be a divorcee? What was it like for me to break apart from my husband whom I had plans of living my whole life with? I had not planned any exit strategy to my marriage. There was no *either or* and *if and then* statements designing my future in the marriage. I had intended to stay in wedlock for life. I wanted to be like my parents who will be celebrating fifty years of marriage this year. I had never thought of a divorce. I dreamed of celebrating my silver and golden years in marriage as well.

What was it like for me to then be judged in such a derogatory manner? What was it like for me to not feel loved?

At this point, what I was going through did not seem to matter at all. I had brought this upon myself. Everyone else knew better. I had failed. A part of me had shut down. I had never known failure before now. Should I have been ashamed and guilty? Should I have continued giving him several chances for the rest of our lives when he was doing his best in overcoming his weaknesses? I did not have any answers.

In 2002, I pulled myself together and went back to school after almost a decade. The Sisters (Loreto nuns) in my school always had my back. They gave me a chance to pursue my teacher's education. Even though I chose to go back, I told myself the story that my brain had rusted and that I may not be able to complete the course. However, I was ready to struggle to go back into being a student again. My post graduate education program became my escape from my experiences at home. It created the space for me to feel good about myself. It was the healing ground for me to rebuild not only my worth and confidence, but my resilience too. My accomplishments motivated me. The professors and fellow students motivated me to be a leader in my life again. Those were the best days of my life. I created new friendship and took on leadership roles. Empowered by appreciation and acknowledgement, I got my life back. I excelled as one of the best student teachers, and showed outstanding results.

My home scenario was a dark contrast. Based on my experiences, I perceived my return to my parents' home as a struggle to retrieve my dignity. I did not feel good about being in the only place that I could ever call my home. Since I was a girl-child, it was ordained that I had to get married and *go away*. What or who was supposedly in the way of *going away* was my precious child. Few men proposed marriage to me. The divorced men did not want a *mother-with-a-daughter combo*, but a wife package only. One of my sisters-in-law had offered to adopt my daughter. I would give up anything in the world to have Sabah stay with me. She was my baby and the love of my life. I would never give her away.

My mom encouraged me to look at matrimonial ads. I went through a roller coaster of experiences. I met men online on matrimonial websites. Swarmed by several responses, I was thrilled and often chuckled at the silliness of some. My ego was having a feast! I was being liked by other human beings even after I was divorced. Common sense told me they were not looking for marriage. Like any other game, this game of life had exceptions too.

One man stood out. The only one from the several men that wasted my time and theirs- he was real and authentic. He was our first experience of a Canadian South-Asian man. He was honest, gracious, respectful, and full of compassion for my daughter. He had a father's heart because he had children of his own and he missed them. He knew the pain of a family falling apart and its impact on children. My child mattered to him.

His kind behaviour stirred my interest. Our long-distance relationship was growing into a daily experience. Azam made his intentions clear. We both agreed to first know each other.

We used MSN messenger for video chats and phone calls to communicate before we met in person later in Canada. A few months went by and his conversations nourished the sparkle back in my eyes. I looked forward to conversations with him. He called me every day and made an effort to know all my family members. He interacted with them as well. He consciously built a relationship with each one of them. Above all he made me laugh! Speaking with him brought ease into my life. He helped me to see life in a lighter perspective.

Living in our joint family implied that *all* walls have ears. Some of these ears have mouths to spread news faster than Reuters ever could. There was a possibility of an overseas relationship brewing here. There were no disclaimers for rumours. My favourite cousin was going to have a grand traditional wedding. This would include elaborate rituals and several days of celebrations. He asked me to invite Azam to create the opportunity for me to meet him in person. It was important to investigate Azam's credibility as a good match for me in a foreign land.

Exercise:

- *Here's something for you to play with.*

- *For a moment, pretend to be an eligible single person even if you are not one.*

- *Write down ten things about yourself that you deeply appreciate.*

Notes:

Enter Sahir

Sahir's sister Maira, (as I had mentioned earlier) was also my father's cousin- Aleph's wife. Even though the men in the family were hostile over property, some of the women shared a congenial space. We heard that Sahir was highly influential and ran a successful immigration business in Canada. We contacted him to enquire about Azam to confirm if he was authentic. Azam and I had been in a long-distance relationship for a year. After a couple of weeks, Sahir called back to inform us that there were red flags. Sahir discouraged us from being in contact with Azam. He said that Azam had been to a Canadian prison. That scared me. I was afraid of being hurt again. I stopped communicating with Azam and never told him why. He was blocked from my contact list.

Being an expert in Canadian immigration matters, Sahir also advised that as a teacher, I was qualified to apply for immigration as a Skilled Worker. It was a good idea to come to a new country on one's own merits and not marry a stranger and immigrate here, he said. I was impressed that he thought differently and felt relieved to not be under any pressure to marry. I liked his advice. On further consultation, he asked me for all my details that were required to complete my paperwork. My divorce documents spelled the reason for my divorce.

The fees for my daughter and I to immigrate to Canada were unaffordable. I dropped the idea of immigrating. There was no urgency or desperation to move to Canada. I had no family there and the cultural difference was a big question. The cold weather was harsh for us who came from a warm and humid country like India. I had people around me in India, a big family that sometimes hurt me, but some of them also kept me distracted from my inner pain. These people were my comfort and helped me to cope with loneliness. I never wanted to be alone. I was born here. For every mean person in the family, there were a few loving ones too.

Additionally, I would not ask my father for any further financial help to migrate to Canada. He had already done enough. He had offered dowry for my first marriage and supported me financially. He hosted us in his home for several years after my divorce. He paid for both Sabah's and my education and for our daily living expenses. I had declined the idea of immigrating to Canada, too scared to venture out alone. Sabah and I had never lived alone. I did not know what it was like to do so. The idea never crossed my mind. I was taught that good women from respectful homes, lived with parents, and then lived as a wife with her husband. Later, she lived with her children. Women never lived alone. So as a woman, how could I ever live alone? I did not know what living alone in a foreign land would imply and the fear of the unknown was dissuading me.

Exercise:

- *Have you ever spent time alone with yourself?*

- *If yes, answer these:*

  - *What was it like for you to be in your own company?*

  - *What did you discover about yourself?*

- *If you have never spent time alone and feel uncomfortable being in your own company, I invite you to do the following:*

  - *Take a walk alone in a park nearby and be present to your thoughts.*

  - *Invite yourself to watch a movie alone. What thoughts cross your mind?*

- *Journal your thoughts.*

- *(When I did this for the first time, I was so miserable and lonely. I did not give up. Over time I have learned to enjoy my own company).*

- *Next: Invite yourself to eat alone at a restaurant. On my first day of eating alone, I was awkward and it felt like all eyes at the restaurant were on me!*

Notes: ✐

_____

_____

_____

_____

_____

_____

_____

_____

_____

_____

_____

_____

_____

_____

_____

_____

No – The Hardest Lesson

The reason for communicating with Sahir had almost reached the end. One day I received an email from him confessing that even though he lived far away in Canada, Sahir was still very much in love with me after so many years had gone by. He had never forgotten me from when he had last seen me at my home. He said that every time he visited his sister in India, he would silently yearn to get a glimpse of me. He expressed that he was incomplete without me.

I remember that moment vividly. I read the email several times just to be sure of what I was reading and my first response to it was, "What a jerk!" I assumed that he was one of those sick married men flirting with a woman in distress. My walls were up. I had already met married men who pretended they were unhappy. I was always wary of married men looking for clandestine relationships.

Sahir was persistent. As I look back in life, I realize that I was so needy for love that I gave in to his intense expressions of it. His courting was persuasive and hard to ignore. He already knew about my first marriage and why it fell apart. He knew what it was like for me to be back home with my parents.

He knew exactly what was needed to rekindle my heart. His sister had told him about me. I had shared details during the conversations over the phone regarding my immigration.

Sahir had some struggles too as he shared with me. His business partnership had fallen apart. He was struggling with accountability to his clients. Sahir said, his partner had robbed him of his clients' money. He had not fulfilled on the contract of ensuring their immigration to Canada. Sahir was left to answer the clients. He requested me to speak with his clients in India. Upon his request, I spoke with his clients and assured them of a fair resolution.

Going back to the moment when my first response nailed him as a jerk – I stopped answering his phone calls. In those days, I had no cell phone. My parents' landline was my only connection. Sahir called me several times each day, and my parents were surprised that I did not want to answer. He kept calling again and again, and my avoidance raised my father's curiosity. I confided in Papa and told him the truth. I let him know about Sahir's email. I was scared and assumed that his love for me was not true. My father encouraged me not to run away or hide, but to face Sahir and say *no*. I think this was the hardest lesson of my life – to be able to say *no,* when something in my gut does not feel right. I was raised in a way where *no* was interpreted as selfish, disrespectful, and rude. I could never say *no* to people because I was a good girl. I wish I had embraced the word *no* as open-mindedly as I do now. *No* is a choice. *No* need not be negative. *No* is a yes to something else. *No* is freedom and *no* is just *no*. It is a complete sentence. I wish I had not just said a feeble *no* to Sahir, but held my ground and made it into a *never*.

Before going to work, I walked to a pay phone booth as we did not have international calling from our home phone. We could only receive international calls. I called Sahir and thanked him for his kind words. Based on what I understood then, I declined his love proposal. The more I said *no*, the harder he proposed. My lips kept saying *no* while my ears betrayed me. They longed to hear the words of love he had to offer me for my future. I was shaking and torn inside. I could not put the phone down. He had such an influence on me; he knew exactly what I had been longing for. Yes I wanted to be loved and to belong in love. Yes. *No.* Yes. *No.* Yes. *No.* Yes. Yes. Yes. I had surrendered. That was the only weak moment of my life. He would not take *no* from me. I went back home and shared my experience with my father and with a cousin I was close to. My cousin suggested that I should get married to him. My father thought that Sahir was a good man and that my daughter, Sabah, would have a good future.

I was scared of being in a far-away land. There were many fears lurking in my head. I had already experienced a failed marriage and was not happy living at my parents' place. There were several setbacks. I needed my own space so that I could seek clarity about what I really wanted. There would be no pressure to get married in order to move out. I was miserable, scared, and confused. I did not know what to do.

On the other hand, there was this man reaching out his hand to hold mine for life. He was so warm and welcoming. He wanted my daughter and me to belong to him just the way I had always wanted. I needed some time to think.

Meanwhile, Sahir had other plans. After 6 months of persuading me he was coming to India by the end of the year. With only 3 months away, he said he wanted me to travel to New Delhi. He wanted me to meet him there so that we could spend a few days *and nights* together. This is how it works in Canada, he said. Coming from a traditional family, I was uncomfortable living with a man out of wedlock. I declined his offer. We had to be married to cohabit. "Till death do us part," he said. I froze. What did he just say? Isn't this my kind of loyal loving? Wasn't that my biggest unrequited wish from my first marriage? He was promising me a future of happily-ever-after from the fairytales.

Sahir wanted to marry me when he came to India. I was panicking at the speed in which he was moving towards me. He was not allowing me any time to think. Those who know Sahir know this about him. He has momentum in his life, and if he wants something, he will do what it takes until he has it. He obsesses over what he wants and tends to become quite irrational. He will not take *no* as an answer and keep pursuing until it becomes a *yes*.

"Please give Shirin to me" he said to my father over the phone. "I want to marry her." Papa knew Sahir's family well. Their mother was a kind Jewish lady. She was fluent in English, and people called her "*Memsaab,*" quite in the colonial tradition.

Rose, as she was called after marriage, had a giving heart. After taking care of 9 children of her own, she would tend to the homeless and poor on the streets of Kolkata. She took them to hospitals when needed and supported them in whatever way she could. She had earned the reputation of being very loving and nurturing. Rose had a fan following amidst the poor. She was also known as a tutor for English to most school children in the neighbourhood.

My father wanted Sahir to send a proper wedding proposal. He wanted Sahir's sister Maira to ask for my hand for Sahir. Sahir rejected the idea. Aleph and papa were in court battles over property matters. Sahir strongly believed that his sister and Aleph would not approve of this relationship. He discouraged us to even mention it to Maira. Sahir asked papa if a formal proposal was of more significance to him than his daughter's and granddaughter's fulfilled future. Papa gave in.

Papa believed that Sahir was a good woman's

son. He must have been raised well and would be a man of integrity. Besides, being older than me by at least a decade, he would be mature and sensible. Most of all, Papa believed that Sahir loved me and that Sabah and I would have a safe and stable life with him. Meanwhile, Sahir already booked his flight tickets and sent me his itinerary. He had plans of stopping over in Dubai and then Karachi to do some shopping for my wedding! While we were still thinking about this, Sahir had already taken action on it.

Notes: ✍

Greed Marries Need

On December 16th, 2003, in a mosque in New Delhi, in a quiet *Nikaah* ceremony, acknowledging the presence of God and amidst witnesses, Sahir took me as his wife. I had to pinch myself. This was really happening. It happened too fast, as if I was under a spell. A voice within me kept saying this was too good to be true yet the experience of being loved by another human being was too hard to ignore. I was so starved of feeling loved and feeling special. From being a *bechaari* (poor thing) to a *bojh* (an encumbrance), I wanted to be back in a space of love and respect that I could call my own home.

My honeymoon was a dream. It restored me and gave me the reassurance that I was loveable. Even though it was a second marriage for both of us, we were oblivious of the rest of the world. We were madly in love with each other. Sahir went on a wish-fulfilling spree. We went to all those places and did all the things that were on *my* dream list. He loved everything about me and paid attention to details. He noticed the polish on my nails to how my hair looked. He noticed everything. I felt visible and important. I loved to see myself as a very beautiful and phenomenal human being that he saw me as. In fact, I did not have such an elevated opinion of myself. My ex-husband had chosen drugs over me and our only child. He was mostly too high on drugs and oblivious of anyone around him. My self-worth was completely destroyed. His actions had destroyed my self-confidence and I would tell myself that I was not good enough.

Sahir loved being loved as well. Unlike Junaid, Sahir was alive. He did not feel fulfilled in his first marriage as he eventually confided in me. The relationship was very demanding on him. He supported his in-laws' immigration to Canada and helped them financially by buying their property in India. He was being compelled to take on financial responsibilities for them. It seemed that he was not just married to Maya, but to her whole family. He felt financially pressured. Sahir always said that he was passionate and self-expressed with me. He could not be so with her, and his marriage suffered. The biggest blow that rocked his previous marriage was the abortion that his ex-wife had had. She always, always had her way, and he said he could not tell her anything.

As our love deepened into a friendship and we continued bonding, he became more open. "Maya made me want to throw up with her obsession for shopping," he said. She came from a mediocre family of Mumbai and loved the riches Sahir had to offer her. She was a stay at home mom and found happiness in shopping and wearing fancy clothes. She loved going on exotic vacations, sending her children to private schools, and living in a fancy mansion. It was all about keeping up with the rich.

The abortion broke his heart. Her parents had moved to Atlanta. She was insisting that he should leave his mother and siblings in Toronto. She was forcing him to leave a thriving family business to move to Atlanta. *Her* need for proximity to *her* parents was more significant to her than his need to be with his family. In fact, her needs and wishes in any matter were always more significant to her than any of his needs and wishes.

When he refused, he said, she was willing to leave without him. She was determined to live with her parents in Atlanta. Even if it meant that Sahir would have to miss being with his first child, Simi. Maya knew Simi was Sahir's weakness. She had her trump card always– her first born– and Maya knew how to use it quickly. Maya always knew how to use her children to prop her relationship with Sahir and keep it going for her. To get her way with him, she gave him the silent treatment for days until he gave in.

Coming back to my story, Sahir married me in India and came back to Canada promising to sponsor me soon. It was hard to be far away from each other. We were in love. I waited patiently in India for my immigration. He visited me seven times to nurture our relationship and called me every day. Sahir had to wait after his separation was a year old to file for divorce. After over a year of patience, we married again as per Canadian law, and Sahir sponsored me to Canada as his wife. Sabah came with me as part of the sponsorship. Life could not have been easier. Patience has its rewards.

Notes: ✍

_____

_____

_____

_____

_____

_____

_____

_____

_____

_____

_____

_____

_____

_____

_____

_____

_____

Oh Canada

On October 25th, 2005, Sabah and I landed in Toronto at the Pearson International Airport. I couldn't wait to be in my own home. I was excited to see the furnished lakeside home with a giant television and double door fridge. Sahir had mentioned these on the phone. He picked us up. I was finally going to be in my own home. I was anticipating a dramatic contrast to the floors I had slept on and the plastic bags that I had lived out of back home in India. My heart was pounding in excitement. I had waited for two years to experience this moment.

The house by the lake was actually an apartment in Parkdale. A prostitute was standing outside making inappropriate gestures at men passing by. I clutched Sabah as we walked past her and went up a flight of steep and narrow stairs inside a store-front house. We stepped into a place that was not what Sahir had been describing to me over the phone for the last two years. As soon as we opened the door, we walked into a hallway that was turned into a mini kitchen. There was a stove, sink, fridge, and two overhead cabinets, much like a bachelor unit. There were two rooms- one had a dining table and four chairs while the other room had a mattress on the floor. A bed frame was propped in the corner. The fridge was filled with six huge cans of orange Tropicana juice.

My blood ran cold as I looked at my daughter's face. This was the beginning of my life in Canada. I had so many questions and I chose to stifle them in my throat. After all, I was a good woman from a good home, the same good woman who couldn't say *no*.

Good women from good homes never ask questions. I was so grateful that he wanted to marry me. He was the *only* one who accepted my daughter as his, and sponsored her with me. He had earned my silence and my surrendering.

However, deep within, I was uncomfortable. Something did not feel right. I did not feel good about the way he welcomed me. There were no sheets on the mattress on the floor. Even though I had an inner feeling that something was wrong, I chose to make myself wrong. I asked my inner voice to hush up.

Sahir took out a flip phone and gave it to me. He said it belonged to his client and I could use it. I could only call him. I could not call India. It was relieving to know that my parents could call me though. And then, to my surprise, he got up and left us alone on our very first evening in Canada. He left us with a promise that he would be back next morning. I went to bed suppressing my feelings and washing them away in my tears. I did not want Sabah to see me cry. I did not sleep that night.

I was not ready for this, and perhaps I will remember this if not grieve about it for the rest of my life. He left me and my daughter alone on the very first night of our arrival in Toronto. Coming home to my first night with my husband meant the world to me. I lived in regret for letting him go. That was the night that made my destiny here in Canada and going forward, I had only occasional nights with him.

As early as 6:00 am, I heard a knock on my door. I looked through the peephole, thinking it must be Sahir. It was Dylan, our neighbour who lived in the only other apartment on the same floor. I had heard of Dylan. Dylan the Painter was a young Jamaican man and Sahir's tenant. I opened the chained door slightly, and the smell of weed rushed to my face. Dylan was upset and I wondered why he called me "Ms. Stein!"

I did not know that Sahir had not paid him for his work. Dylan wanted to come in and take away the dollar store shower curtain that he had put up for us. My face flushed in embarrassment, I requested for him to come when Sahir was home. This yet another new experience for me.

Sahir came home in the morning. In the relief and excitement of a new day with him, I did not want to start with complaining. We were going for a drive with Sahir to see Toronto in our car!

For the first two weeks, as a ritual, Sahir began to come home every morning and leave in the evenings. He took us for long drives and we ate outside. We were living like we were on a vacation! Sabah and I were exploring Canada. Everything was so different, and we were wrapped in the experience of being in a new place. We felt rich and grateful for being able to buy our own groceries. This was *my* home and the groceries were what *I* wanted. After all, it had been over five years of living their way in other peoples' homes.

Be happy with little, never ask for things. These were rules to live by for good women from good homes. Marry a man for his love and never want to own his money- that is being slutty. Good women from good homes were an embodiment of sacrifice and martyrdom. After all, my grandmother was the best woman on this planet. Part of how good she was included her ability to sacrifice. She ought to be good. She gave away her life, her abundance, to everybody. She died fully spent with not a complaint or regret on her lips. She lived her entire life raising her 13 children. Some disabled and some struggling with their lives. She took on their troubles as hers. She had room for more. She went on a spree helping others in the family too. She was my role model. Don't people glorify martyrs? I wanted to be like her.

No one likes a woman who can be a stand for something. No one likes a woman who has a voice. Good girls from good homes are never heard. Where did I hear that again? Oh yes, in Sahir's family. Women who were invisible and silently suffered are the treasures of the family. Victim life is validating!

Going back to our first two weeks in Canada, Sabah was already in school, and we were learning to get used to what life would look like for us in Canada. We were doing all the paperwork and applied for the various "cards" that would make us Canadian.

It was lonely when Sahir left. We saw our evening skies turn into night skies from our windows. We were scared to go out alone and had no television to entertain us. I would often wonder where was the big television that Sahir told me he was buying for us while we were in India. I never asked. Dylan was our only neighbour and I was afraid to interact with him. Coming from my past experiences, I did not want to trouble. This place had a different culture from India. I was afraid of making a mistake and getting into trouble in a new country.

By mid-November, Sahir decided to move his office to our home and he asked Dylan to leave. Dylan's apartment turned into Sahir's office. From then on, I began my new avatar as Sabrina Moses.

Why Sabrina Moses? I was going to be in Sahir's office as his Secretary, Office-Administrator, and Janitor – one in all. When an Altaf comes to North America, he becomes Al, he said. It's easier for North Americans to remember and pronounce his name. Likewise, a Sundeep becomes Sandy and Shirin becomes Sabrina. So I gave up my name to fit in.

Sabrina's career turned out to be a very successful one. She was ambitious and eager to learn. She picked up the business tactics of an Immigration Consultant. She took it to a whole new level of learned and informed practice. Sabrina studied for it while Sahir had the license to practice it. She encouraged and motivated Sahir to study law and become an Immigration Lawyer. Sahir was not inclined towards academic pursuits. Sahir's appreciation was Sabrina's only compensation.

She remained a woman from India, educated, and still believing that her husband should handle her finances. It was perfectly alright with her to not own or have access to any money. After all she was used to a culture where men gave women a couple of bills to go and buy what they wanted. That's it. Good girls from good homes do not go out to work. They are stay-at-home women. Sahir always assured me that everything he earned was ours and for our children. He knew I was not demanding, and he encouraged that.

Deep within, it was challenging for me because I earned my own money as a teacher in India. Despite that, I pushed myself to live with no money. My pride never allowed me to ask him for it. In January of 2006, Sahir gave me my first hundred dollars as pocket money. I waited two and a half months for that. By that time, we had a long list of needs that came with our first winter in Canada and with Sabah having started school in the fall. We had no clothes that would keep us warm enough in our very first Canadian snowy winter experience. I still remember Sabah going to school in sneakers. I wonder why she did not ever say a word about how cold she must have been. Her mittens, hats and scarves were from the dollar store. That's what I could afford. They were not always warm enough for extreme weather.

I did not know how to dress up in the winter here. I did not know anything about what snow pants were. What were waterproof boots? How to dress in temperatures of minus 30 and 40 degrees? Life had taught Sabah early in life to stay quiet. As strange as it may sound, we had no friends to tell us how to live here. Sahir was our only human connection in Canada. He kept us busy in the day, and we were too scared to venture out when he left.

I grew up believing that money causes conflicts. I could never ask Sahir for money and we suffered.

One day, to my surprise, Azam (the man from the matrimonial website) called me on my phone! He had called my parents' home in India to enquire about me. They informed him that I married Sahir and was living in Canada. Azam invited us to his beautiful cottage in Aurora. This was the first time I met Azam in person, and he later continued to regret having lost me. He seemed to be a decent person. Azam was very Happy to meet Sabah and spoiled her with her first winter wear in Canada. Now I had a friend to talk to in Canada.

"Come away with me," said Azam.

He offered to marry me and give me a more fulfilling life. My loyalty lay with Sahir and, to me, this was not acceptable. I rejected Azam's friendship and withdrew into my own closed world with Sahir. Sahir was very possessive of me and did not like the idea of me having any connection with Azam. At that time, what Sahir liked, mattered the most. I saw his controlling nature as immense love and thought it would hurt him.

Sahir always took pride in the fact that he wanted a big family. He already had children from his first wife and wanted more. He always said that he had 10 brothers and sisters, and wanted 10 children too. Although I was not ready for that number, I did want my own children with him. The stress began when I did not get pregnant for the first 6 months of being here. He was upset and began to accuse me for it. He believed that I must be evil if I did not bear children and the pressure of that accusation began to disturb my mind. I was not evil, and every night I would lay awake in bed stressing over getting pregnant. His words– "If I walk past any woman, I can get her pregnant. What is wrong with you?" kept playing over and over again on my mind. I began to feel anxious and believed that something was wrong with me. A visit to the doctor did not help as she thought I was healthy and making stress a natural birth control.

The more he called me evil and unlucky, the more insecure I became. I began to demand that he should stay at home every evening. Then my insecurities made me more demanding and argumentative. I was afraid and demanded Sahir's full support to make me feel secure and loved. Instead, he called up my cousin in the USA and asked him to take me away. He also called my father and said he was done with me. I could go back to India.

That was a big emotional blow for me. I was ashamed and embarrassed to include my cousin in this sensitive family matter. No one had ever complained about me to my family. I did not know where to hide. I shut down emotionally. Succumbed in the mere thought of what people would say, instead of going back, I made myself wrong. I chose a known life of suffering and humiliation. I did not want a life of being alone and without a partner to love me. I did not want a life of condemnation.

That day, I chose abuse over a life of dignity. I had repressed anger within me, anger towards myself. Why was I choosing this life of pain, shame, and humiliation for myself? Once again, I surrendered to the idea that I was not good enough. It took me a mortal threat to break that spell after over seven years of living as a victim, to change that later.

Notes: ✍

The Story of a Broken Smile

It was Friday April 14th, 2006. I was almost six months into moving to Canada. Life was not as promised. I was under a lot of stress. Unpleasant surprises awaited me at every bend. "If you don't like it, go back to India," he often yelled. Ultimatums and deadlines seemed to control my everyday life. I felt like a prisoner or worse still, a slave. These thoughts bombarded my mind. I was walking back to the subway station to go back home, or should I say, to go back to my prison. A home is not a trap you can't seem to get out of. I wish I could run away, but I had my little 10-year-old silently watching the predator and victim game. Her silence boomed loud in my head - Do something! The April rain washed my face and mingled with my tears. I plodded home that day to experience the worst.

As I looked in the mirror, the right side of my face began to droop. I looked like I was mocking, and I had no control over the shape of my mouth. My right eye wouldn't blink and seemed to have frozen open. My little girl looked at my face and said something is wrong with it. I went into panic mode.

Was it a heart attack? Was I dying?

I had no one here other than my little daughter. What would become of her if I were to die? The thoughts were driving me insane with anxiety. I lay down quietly in bed and prayed to keep myself calm until it was early morning. Sahir did not come until then.

I had never been to a hospital in Canada, and my first experience in the Emergency Room was frustrating. It was overcrowded with patients. Not before afternoon a doctor saw me and said I had Bell's palsy. What on earth was that! I had never heard of it. I knew there was palsy as in Cerebral palsy. Did I do myself some kind of a brain damage? After all I was extremely stressed and had no one to talk to. There was no assurance that my face would go back to how it was and there was no predictable time frame in which it would. There was no specific medication that could cure it. Steroids could work, but there was no surety. My seventh cranial nerve was paralyzed.

My smile was the brand of my being. Now my smile was broken. I hated looking at myself in the mirror. It was a cruel lesson in self-acceptance and self-love.

I became too ugly for him. "I am not used to ugly faces, fix it." He said. "It runs in your family, you had aunts and uncles who had deformed bodies. I am not used to it."

He was right. I did have uncles and aunts who were disabled. I grew up in total acceptance of their physical disabilities. I grew up as a child believing that human beings could look different. I never saw them disempowered though. They made significant contributions to our family. They shared their talents and skills and often took on leadership roles in the family. In fact, my heart fills with gratitude for them. They enabled me powerfully to be sensitive and resilient, they were my heroes. Most of my talents in art and craft and cooking come from them. They were one of the most powerful and resilient members of our family. Most of all, they were extremely enabled in showering us with their love. My powers and talents are from them. They were super-abled.

It was only with Sahir that for the first time in my life I experienced a disempowered context around the word *disability*. I was now on the other side of the spectrum of ability. My paralysis had disabled me and I had a husband who was communicating his disapproval. I began to feel that I was no longer a normal, enabled person.

Something was wrong with me. Something was wrong with all those disabled aunts and uncle. We were all misfits in society, the society of people like my husband. My spirit curled up like the petals of a withering flower and I wanted to become invisible.

Notes: ✍

The Second Wife

Despite being his wife, I was reduced to slavery or, should I say, seduced into slavery. Sahir continued to maintain relationship with his ex-wife. This left me to struggle for my rights as a second wife in Canada. While I had no children from him, Sahir had two more from Maya after we got married. My fears and Sahir's verbal abuse were magnifying my feelings of low self-worth. I was already ugly with the paralysis. I began to feel that I did not deserve anything better than what Sahir had to offer me as my life partner. I began to believe that I was not loveable and gave in to his atrocities.

During one episode of verbal and emotional abuse, I mustered the courage to warn Sahir. That day, something took over me, and I do not know from where in my inner knowing I got this. I turned around and told Sahir with conviction that I *would* give birth and that I would have twins. "You watch," I said. "I will make up for the two years that I did not get pregnant and I will have twins. I am not evil, God loves me." I do not know where in my being this came from. I was hurt and agonized, and this was my cry of suffering.

Truly enough, in the fall of 2007, I gave birth to twins, a girl and a boy – my own children from Sahir. I was relieved that there was proof, I was not evil and God does love me. Maya continued to take over as his partner and I continued to live my life second class. By 2010, I was a citizen of Canada and had given birth to my youngest daughter from Sahir. Our marriage dragged in the ebb and flow of a love-hate relationship. I kept compromising.

What did being a second wife look like for me?

Sahir never admitted to his family and to his congregation that I was his wife and that my three younger children were his. We got to keep his first name as our last name while Maya and her four children owned his last name.

I was office secretary, property manager, janitor, tutor, cook, laundry service provider and his personal masseuse. Maya got to own all the money that came from my hard work and sacrifices. The properties and cheque books had her name aside his.

I got to keep the responsibilities while she owned the fruits of my labour.

Our evenings, nights, and weekends were all spent alone. On festivals and holidays we were alone. She was entitled to every vacation and celebration.

I struggled to put together $2,000 for a needle that I needed for my cancer surgery while she gave away thousands-of-dollars in charity to her distant relatives and acquaintances. I ended up having cancer.

I will share that episode of my life later in this book.

I got to live in his office, and she owned a seven-bedroom mansion in a posh neighbourhood.

My daughter Sabah worked all night at McDonalds. She worked to pay for her undergraduate education. She went to school exhausted every morning. Maya's daughter was driving her own car to high school and going on shopping dates with her friends.

It sucked being a second wife, or should I say, being a slave.

More importantly, Maya was seen as the *poor thing* and the victim in Sahir's family. I was judged as the wicked home-wrecker. Maya was silently enjoying the victory of usurping who and what should have been part of *our* lives. There was no way I would ever stand a chance against the context I had created around myself.

I was always the second choice, the lower than, lesser than. "Our allegiance is to her," said his younger brother to me. "We had brought her into the family." His sister called me a *vulture* and Sahir remained silent to cover up his lies. He never owned up to having created this mess. When they needed problem-solving, they chose me over her. At that time their allegiance to her wavered. Conveniently, that relationship was restored as soon as I had finished serving them. Every time, they used Sahir to convince me. Sahir always said, "If you take care of them, my family will love you." I was willing to bury my pride to be loved. I wanted to be included and acknowledged by Sahir's family. They knew that.

I fulfilled all their unreasonable requests. They requested coaching and empowering his nieces- I coached them. Maira requested that I buy Maira's trinkets from India- I bought them. She would bring loads of them to make money while she visited Canada.

Night after night I lay in bed questioning my faith. I questioned the religious books, questioned what equal and fair treatment was. I re-lived my traumatizing memories. When he came home to tell me how Maya looked better and dressed better than me and shared with me details of how he had intimacy with her, my heart would sink with the comparisons, and I would rather have been dead in those moments.

When he shared with me the way he spent his moments with her, there were no filters. I began to resent Maya. He was clearly very demanding of me, and I felt abused. I couldn't sleep at night. I tossed in bed for years, in mental and emotional agony, imagining what he must be doing with Maya at that time. I did not reach out to anyone for help. I was scared and ashamed and knew I was destroying myself. I could feel the energy of a volcano of negative emotions building up inside me, and I was bound to erupt.

I grew more frustrated as Sahir discussed

Maya, and showed me photos of the latest fun times with her. I could never ever justify the callousness of the woman who enjoyed what was ours, knowing we were suffering. She knew it was ours, and that I had worked hard for it. She had gotten news of our marriage even before Sahir had reached India to marry me. She knew he had bought our wedding bands and got my initials inscribed on them. My cousin Gizel had let her know. Being in denial was advantageous for her.

Another sad experience was Sahir's birthday. We got to be bystanders and she got to celebrate it with pomp and show. Maya had her friend blog about her great love story with a man whom she knew very well was now mine. She invited us to the party while Maira, my aunt, asked us to stay away. I felt wronged, frustrated, and angry. When would I ever have the chance to do a first of anything with him? In the little time we had together, I was forced to discuss work or be ridiculed, taunted and verbally abused.

Sahir came up with several stories with the greatest ease. It was habitual for him to distort the truth so that it worked for him. He claimed I was a beggar on the streets of Kolkata. He claimed to be the epitome of magnanimity to have given me a life in Canada. He became a self-proclaimed hero to his family, especially to Maya. Sahir would cruelly suggest to his family that I was delusional that he was my husband. He had lied to Maya that I had a boyfriend who lived in USA, and that the three younger children were not his. My son looks exactly like Sahir!

From one lie to another, he was on a binge. He was not willing to take responsibility for his actions and dumped all the blame on me.

Another version of his story went like this, he never loved me. My father begged him to marry me. He was a magnanimous philanthropist who put his marriage at stake so that I could immigrate to Canada. There were as many versions of his story as there were people in his family who questioned him.

If he did not love me and that was true, I wondered why he gave me a house to live in and a place to work for him? Why did he have three children with me?

Why was it so difficult for Maya to not see through his lies? Why did she spin a tale that I took advantage of him? She wrote once that I had enticed him into having children while he came to me for office work only. Not one, not two, but three children- a result of enticing him? I kept on enticing him and he kept visiting me to be enticed? My mind was flooded with question after question that I could not find answers to. These questions would not stop. They would not leave me in peace. The monkey chatter made a lot of noise in my mind. It would not let me sleep.

I reached out to his family members several times. For every truth I screamed out loud, he stifled my voice with heaps of lies while his family watched in silent support of him. His family remained bystanders, choosing to believe in his lies to suit their convenience. They had a lot at stake. They were scared to lose all their money that they had loaned him for his real estate business.

Exercise:

- *Many of us have some kind of monkey chatter. Do you have any? What is it saying?*

- *What negative thoughts flood your brains?*

- *Identify them and make a list of them*

- *Create positive affirmations that negate these negative thoughts.*

- *For example, if the noisy and disturbing nay saying voice inside your head tells you that you are not good enough, write beside it "I am awesome".*

- *Every time that negative thought switches on in your mind, consciously affirm with a positive sentence.*

- *Reprogram your mind to positivity, one sentence at a time.*

Notes: ✍

Raising Abuse

Sahir had no respect for women. He would share the tales of malicious gossip he heard from my parents' house. Even though Aleph, my uncle, had died, Maira continued to live there as his widow.

Sahir often claimed to have updates on my father's affluence. "He never gave you any dowry. In a way he sold you to me." Over and over again, it would be the same vitriolic taunts. It seemed like he was holding me for ransom so that his sister could extort as much property as she could from Papa. She reaped the financial benefits that came from our relationship.

Sahir seemed to be seeking accountability from me for what my father was doing or not doing in his own family. My life was tortuous, he was very controlling. I dreaded my aunt turned sister-in-law, Maira, when she visited Toronto. She began to visit here and her presence was felt in the bitterness and nastiness of my husband. Sahir expressed his anger towards my parents and eventually became nasty with me. Sahir's ugly taunting would herald her arrival to Canada. She brought out the dragon in him, a dragon who was ready to spit fire at me. The remote of this fire-spitting dragon was in Maira's hands. Sahir became unrecognizably monstrous, brutally bitter and viciously vulgar.

He would say, "That was how a man treats his wife who was not a virgin when he married her. You did not bring any dowry." I would often wonder, virgin or mother, both are sacred states of being for a woman. Where was the comparison? Sahir never liked my ability to still be able to think and though weakly, stand up for myself. It threatened him. He wanted to destroy my spirit.

Sahir was a *man*, a *rich man*. I was a divorcee, a single mother of a child (to be read as baggage). I was not a virgin when he married me, so I deserved the life that Sahir was offering.

Sahir still came home every morning and left every evening. He controlled the way I looked, what we ate, and what we wore. He controlled where we went, who we spoke to and what we did every day when he lived with us and even when he did not. No matter how hard I tried, there was always something missing for him to appreciate me. It was never good enough. On the other hand, whatever he did, he bragged about it with exaggeration.

As our business expanded, Sahir became even more controlling and cruel. He was conceited and obnoxiously vulgar. He bragged about being able to get any girl he wanted. He was in total acceptance of the idea of men abusing women. After all he had seen his father abuse his mother. He had witnessed most of his sisters being abused by their husbands, and that is what he knew was a manly thing to do. In his family, suppressing women was being *macho*.

It did not take much time for me to deteriorate and succumb to his daily dose of verbal violence. Calling me ugly and not good enough was not enough. I began to look the worst and withdrew from the few people I knew. I did not feel good about being in my skin. I wanted to hide from everybody. Those were years of tremendous suffering. I did not feel good about myself, and it was hard to accept who I had become.

Sahir didn't quite see his behaviour as abuse. What was abuse for me was his normal. He would share stories of his paternal grandmother throwing hot water at his own mother. She would also rub chillies in his mother's eyes for being a daughter-in-law from a different community. To Sahir, his mother was an angel for silently putting up with all these atrocities.

Often, he compared himself with his father and said that his father would get drunk and beat his mother. Since Sahir was a teetotaller and never beat me, he claimed that he was better than his father. He was only impacting my mental health, that didn't matter. For his family, it was normal for the men to misuse power and authority to hurt others. He was the ninth of ten siblings, and he knew that some of his sisters were beaten by their husbands. He often shared the memories he had of all the abuse he witnessed in his family. Most of all, as a child he would get severely beaten and lashed with a belt by his older sister for any mistakes he made. He grew up in abuse. This was a normal experience for some of us who grew up in India a few decades ago. Parenting strategies were governed by the rod. Beating children was a part of the regime of raising them well.

It was shocking to discover the acceptance of abuse amongst the women in his family. Men abused women and women abused their children as part of family culture. The girls of the family naturally accepted abuse as a way of life. The men were raised to be disrespectful to the women. Abuse was their muscle of power. The women in his family embraced abuse because they were women - as if it was wrong to be born as one. They were not proud women. They believed they would earn a place in heaven for silently putting up with abuse from their men. They exalted and honoured women who did not raise their voices against abuse. In fact, how much abuse a woman could silently bear was a measure of how good they were as human beings! Abuse was their way of being and a hand-me-down from one woman to another. They did not know any other way. They definitely did not like me because just before I had cancer, I could not take the abuse anymore and began to retaliate.

I was never beaten by my father. The men in our family never raised their hands on the women. It was very hard for me to accept Sahir's normal as my normal. Sahir classified the men in my family as wimps for not having that ugly control over their women. Sahir justified that he was not indulging in physical violence and I never got his world. He was always afraid of being classified as "hen-pecked." He was under pressure to ill-treat me in order to be validated by his sisters. In fact, his sisters approved of his abusive nature and indulged him.

While I was growing up in India, I was confident in expressing and voicing my opinions against dowry. I took a stand for gender equality when I was a teenager in high school. As a victim of emotional and mental abuse, I admit that he burnt holes of negative feelings in my mind. I hated myself and wanted to die. It was very stressful, intimidating, and exhausting to be his wife. What to him was merely yelling and swearing to assert his manliness was serious torture for me. I spent several nights in bed, alone and crying. I re-lived the verbal, mental, and emotional holocaust. My mind became a battlefield. Being still in love with Sahir, I looked for shallow excuses to justify his behaviour. I was fighting against everything I stood for. I was facing a breakdown in my natural tendency of being loving and gentle to him and his family.

What was eye opening for me was learning that some of us, women, are quick to blame the men. We need to first confront the fact that sometimes some women hurt women more. At first, I was hurt and upset. As I look back, I realize that some women think they do not deserve more. They do not believe in women's rights and freedom. They think they are inferior as if it is very wrong to be a woman. These women are not supportive of women who have an independent voice. They do what has been done to them and the vicious cycle of abuse continues. I have been hurt and shockingly disappointed by women in Sahir's family. They have been instrumental to the way Sahir showed up later in my life and in the breakdown of our marriage.

Towards the last few years of my marriage, I went into survival mode. By then I had already developed cancer and was frustrated, angry, and very reactive. I would retort with even more verbal abuse every time Sahir attacked me verbally. I would feel compelled to call or email his brothers, sisters, and Maya. Sick of the abuse and his never ending lies, the monster in me was unleashed in sheer rebellion, and I became my most bitter and ugly self. I had had enough of being sworn at and I began to lash out. The floodgates of pain and suffering that I had contained within me burst open. What flowed through my tongue were some of the worst verbal expressions of my being. I had hit rock bottom. I was experiencing my own inferno. There were terrible shouting matches at home. Sahir had damaged my mental and emotional health in a very negative manner.

As ridiculous as it may sound, I was exhausted from living my life in such a heightened manner. I wanted to save my marriage and start a new chapter of healthy boundaries and mutual respect. I wished for a fulfilling and happy life with Sahir. I wanted the Sahir who had courted me when I was in India and loved me hard into accepting him as my husband.

In that moment of vulnerability and desperation, I gave up my power to anybody who offered a solution to make my marriage work. I wanted to fix all my problems in a way that did not harm anyone. I blamed Maya, Maira, and even the stars for the breakdown of the relationship.

I wanted those moments back that I once enjoyed with my beloved husband. I sought advice from Sahir's older brother and as guided, spoke with Sahir and Maya's daughter, Simi, about what Sahir had done to me. I had resorted to chanting and conducting expensive elaborate karma cleaning rituals. I would do anything to save my marriage even if it meant soaking myself into financial debt to get these elaborate relationship healing rituals done.

In my desperation to heal our marriage, I discovered Past Life Regression Therapy. An interesting context of Karmic relationship was discovered between Sahir and me. As I regressed into a deep hypnotic state of consciousness, I revived a memory from my past life. Sahir was a cruel king of a kingdom in Africa, and I was the beloved queen of his neighbouring kingdom. Sahir was in love with me while I was in love with another king. I did not love Sahir and had refused his hand in marriage. Sahir had me killed by his most faithful slave. That slave from that past life was Maya in this lifetime, and she had shot a poisoned arrow at my throat. Together, they had killed me in that lifetime. I had to forgive them to clear karma and restore my marriage. Thereafter, I must have chanted as many forgiveness prayers as the number of breaths I take in a day. And nothing worked. No prayers or mantras worked.

I gave in to the demons inside me. I began to tell myself that I was not worthy and that I deserved less. Those were the darkest years of my life. I hated myself and wanted to hide. He was not there to give me a hand as I was overloaded with the responsibility of raising four children alone. I did not care if I had not showered or combed my hair. I had no one to please anyways. I would never be good enough for him. There was no one to notice. However, I did have to show up sound and stable for my children. That was a blessing in disguise, as hard as it might have been sometimes, the habit of putting my children before me saved my life and later gave me a new way of being.

I was emotionally starved of love and missed hearing words of kindness. As I was walking to the convenience store on my block, one day, a homeless man said to me, "Sweetheart, do you have change for coffee?" I stood still to soak in the word *sweetheart*. I had not heard an endearing word in a long time, and I became aware of how emotionally deprived I was of feeling loved.

Exercise:

- *Here is something for you to do.*

- *Sit in front of a mirror for 5 minutes and speak with yourself in a nurturing and loving way.*

- *What would you say to yourself?*

- *Practice this every day for 5 days and build it up to 15 minutes of sitting time.*

Notes:

To Die or Not to Die

I was pushed to the edge of my being. I contemplated death over and over again. It was the only way I could have relief from my internal state of suffering. I was desperate for relief.

One evening, I sat in the washroom with the lights turned off. I was clenching a fist full of pills instead of holding on to life. I was frustrated, exhausted, and depleted of any positivity. Death was freedom; Freedom from living a life of no integrity; Freedom from frustration, pain, humiliation, suffering, and shame. I was ashamed of myself. I was ashamed that I was willing to be a slave just to feel loved and to belong. I was ashamed of myself for compromising on my own personal standards. I was ashamed of living a life of no integrity. Most of all, I was ashamed of how bitter and verbally vulgar I had become. Integrity to me was living a life of alignment to my personal standards. I believed that I was ugly and not good enough. My naturally loving and nurturing disposition was destroyed.

I felt wronged, used, and exploited by Sahir and his family. I had failed over and over again and I thought Maya and Maira were the reasons. I was a loser and it was better to die. In the midst of these dark thoughts of death, I got present to the joyful squeals of my children and I stopped to think.

What would become of my children if I gave up on myself? What would their lives be like? What legacy would I leave behind for them? How would death set me free if after I died and my children grew up to abuse others or be abused instead?

Notes: ✍

Choosing Cancer

The next three years of my life were even more restless times. Sahir and I spent less time together. He moved his office out of our house. He did not need to come home anymore as he did not need me for his business. He had invested all his earnings from his Immigration business to real estate. He did not need me to collect his rent anymore, he could do that himself. He could also afford a property manager to look after his growing real estate business. He came to me when he needed some work done. He came to use and to abuse me.

I had leaned on Sahir for love. I did so because he came to ask for my hand. Back home in India, I had left behind the community of a large joint family. I missed my family, siblings, uncles, aunts, cousins, and grandparents. He was my "everything." His relationship with me was based on a promise of love and trust. Without him, I was lonely and too scared to be left alone with my children in Canada. I had no one here, and I belonged to no one. I had never lived alone. I was afraid to be so.

Sahir had two families. Even though I was legally his wife, he did not honour me as one. I did not feel like his wife. I was his wife on paper. On the other hand, Sahir had divorced Maya, but he continued to honour her. She posed as the silent martyr, the victim, tolerating every atrocity. I was the rebellious, unconventional, and wannabe silent martyr who failed at it. This was an overwhelming truth, and the more I tried to suppress this truth, the uglier it got for me.

I began to intercept every lie that Sahir said to manipulate through his own maze. This infuriated him. He had a cover for every single lie I busted or maybe he didn't. What he really had was a whole family and Maya to back him up no matter what. I was alone. No one liked me. They felt confronted as they had no answer when I called out on a lie. I was reaching out for justice in the family and in the hopes that there would be someone to take a stand. Of all the people in the family, I had the most expectations of Maya, she was a woman who knew the exact truth and chose not to stand up for it. Why could she not see through his lies? I questioned her integrity for choosing his lies over my truth. How was her marriage working anyways? I realized that his lies didn't rock her world and my truth did. Perhaps she did know he lied but she pretended she didn't. Her luxurious life style was at stake and she wouldn't definitely lose that for me and my children. She had children too who were used to a fancy lifestyle.

My wounded spirit groaned, and I went from seeking family to seeking justice. Sahir began to brainwash me into believing that I was mentally ill and convinced me to take medication. He threatened to take all my children away from me and send me back if I did not put up with his ways. His lies and threats became more and more creative.

Eventually, what rocked my being was the tsunami of words that came from him. I had clarity that I wanted separation. Our issues had reached the table of a mediator, and Sahir claimed that he never loved me. I could not lie to myself and pretend being loved by him anymore as I was hearing this straight from his mouth. At first, he even denied that the children were his! Upon further interrogation, he admitted to being the father of my children. But he continued to deny being married to me.

After a while, he admitted that he married me. However, he tagged his story in a way to make him look like a knight in shining armour. His version of the story depicted me as the siren that he went to rescue thinking I was a damsel in distress. Maya and his family chose to buy that story because it kept intact the bubble they were living in.

My world was devastated.

I was falsely accused by Maya of taking advantage of a kind man like Sahir whose only intention was to help me. He married me only to help me to come to Canada, she said. He gave me a roof over my head and a job as a magnanimous gesture because she thought he was a kind man.

Giving me three children were even greater acts of kindness that he claimed and she accepted. He had given them to me because I had no one here and they were my old age security. I could have never felt more disempowered and humiliated.

I am divorced, and very clear about my marital status, though I often wonder about Maya. Is her marriage true? Sahir continues to make indecent proposals to me in the hope that I would agree to have a secret relationship with him. On many occasions he asked to come home while the children were in school. He ignores my refusal and attempts to make the same request again and again. I have learned to not only say no, but to stick to my grounds and to choose myself. I deserve better.

How many women live their lives pretending to be happily married? Do they celebrate milestone anniversaries to *look good* as a couple? How many are married all for show? How many women hush up the betrayals and intrigues in their married life? How many women keep up the pretences for their parents or their children to believe a lie? What is the payoff in being so inauthentic?

My question to you when you lie to your children is, what legacy are you leaving behind for your children? You paint a very perfectly inauthentic picture of life to your children. Do you empower them? Imagine the disservice a woman does to herself when she sells out on herself? She trades the fear of facing pain, shame, and humiliation for *faking* to be happy. Does anyone ever get to see her authentic and vulnerable self?

The patterns repeat for generations. This brings suffering whether they remain married or get divorced. By allowing a man in our family to go on an emotional rampage, how are we a stand for the sanctity of being women? Our silence and passive by-standing can be fatal to other women. Silence breeds abuse. I urge you to awaken and arise.

Around those very turbulent times, a lump had manifested in the left side of my clavicle. Twice, I had coughed up blood. My physical health was the last thing on my mind; I had stopped nurturing myself anyway. I stopped eating and couldn't sleep for several nights. I was contemplating death. I would rather die than go back to India and put my children through the prejudice we had faced once before. My children were my only *raison d'être*.

I had begun to feel sick and lightheaded and had to be rushed to the hospital in an ambulance. My children watched anxiously while the paramedics took me on the stretcher. The doctor suggested that I wait to see if the lump was an oversized lymph node caused by the recent flu.

As I continued working towards a separation from Sahir, my physical health deteriorated. An ultrasound led to escalate concerns of cancer. Several other tests and scans determined that I had metastatic Papillary Thyroid Cancer. It had spread to my lymph nodes.

The doctors had assured me that this kind of cancer was easy to cure. But the cancer cells were aggressive tall cell variants and we had to work harder though. I was in stage 3/4 and needed surgery.

November 27th, 2014 was the day of my surgery. Until that day, Sahir had not given me any assurance about what life would be like for the children should I die. He was still struggling with the terms and conditions of the separation and not willing to let go of his money. Suddenly, just for me, he became one of the busiest men I have ever known. He had no time to stay for my surgery at the hospital. He was too busy to even connect with his humanity. He came to sign the papers for emergency contact person out of sheer obligation and left, constantly cribbing how late he was to work that day. There was nothing else to look to him for. He showed no compassion.

The night before was the hardest for me and my children. It was harder than facing cancer. My children were heartbroken. I was their only parent who showed up for them in every aspect of their lives. I never missed any concerts, children's events, and school nights, birthdays, or play dates. Meanwhile, Sabah's whole life had crumbled further. She was still working at a fast food restaurant to fund her undergraduate studies. She quit her job and dropped out of University. She couldn't focus on anything. Sabah was scared of what her future looked like with imagining me gone and the three siblings left to her. She had turned twenty just a month before.

In the Operating Room, while the anaesthesia was being administered, I experienced a pivotal moment. I accepted that Sahir did not love me. That was the most powerful, life-changing moment of my life.

I had my four beautiful children on my mind, and before I passed out for the surgery, I asked God to give me one chance to live. In that moment, I chose life. Cancer was my gift. It gave me life. It saved me from choosing death; it saved me from living a life I did not want to live and from dying every day. It created the urgency in me to be alive and to choose to live with power and intention.

My greatest purpose became the prevention of abuse from sneaking its way into our children's lives. I wanted to proof my children from the legacy of abuse.

Before I had cancer, I was not living a life that I chose. I was living my life in default. Living by the rules of what comes in sequel-study, education, marriage and children. I remained stuck to the beaten track of life that others around me had trail blazed. I did not know any better.

I was living on deadlines-formal education must end by my early twenties. I should be married and become a mother by my mid- twenties. After I got divorced, I should get married again because I am too young to be celibate and single in my early thirties. I should have all my children before my forties. If I did not live by my husband's rules, I would be deported and my children would be snatched away from me. The list goes on. I was living my life on ultimatums given by others. I was unhappy and not at all cherishing my life. I had a lot of repressed anger and I blamed others for everything that went wrong in my life.

I thought learning to say *no* was a tough lesson in my life, but Cancer was the most powerful lesson of life. No amount of formal education or degrees could teach me what cancer taught me, it cracked me open. It was a life-changing lesson in self-love. I chose to learn this lesson at the cost of almost losing my life. I am so grateful for this lesson. Experiencing cancer awakened my love for myself. It also awakened in me gratitude for life and for the people I encountered along the way. In fact, it was an intense course on several life lessons.

According to the doctor's report, the risks of the surgery included "recurrent nerve injury with associated voice change." It also included "permanent hypoglycaemia, spinal accessory nerve injury, and shoulder weakness." My surgery was successful and none of those happened except for a slight voice change. There was no nerve injury.

After the surgery, the oncology surgeon's

report on my Metastatic Papillary Thyroid Cancer detailed that the operation entailed a total thyroidectomy, and a bilateral central neck dissection. It also included a re-implantation of left inferior parathyroid gland.

He also mentioned that I had a "rock hard" mass in the middle of the thyroid gland, almost as hard as a tennis-ball. "The jugular vein draped over the top of the tumour." And there were very bulky lymph nodes "like a bunch of grapes". He reported that the vagus nerve and carotid artery were not involved in the disease.

"The patient tolerated the procedure well. She returned to the recovery room in satisfactory condition." My sense of gratitude will never allow me to take this sentence lightly. It gave me the credentials of a survivor.

I preserve this report as a testimony of the countless miracles that happened in my life at that crucial time. I must admit that Dr. H., my oncologist, has a graceful healing presence. When I met him for the first time, I knew that I was safe in his hands. His medical acumen and expertise were exceptional. I was intentional in empowering him with my complete trust. When he said, "You will be alright," I chose to believe it.

Exercise:

- *Write yourself an obituary and read it aloud.*

- *If today was the last day of your life, what would you feel about the way you have lived your life so far?*

Notes:

Sabah's Silence

Parallel to what I was experiencing in my life, my little daughter had her own experiences to lament on.

What was it like for my child to be in a new country? What was it like for her to be in a new school? What was it like for her to have a stepfather who had no time or love for her? A man who had no interest in being a nurturing adult in her life?

Before she came to Canada with me, Sabah was spoilt by my father. She felt alone here. I was no longer available to sit with her every day to play games on the computer and giggle over silly things. Leisure time was a luxury and became a part of nostalgic memory. My life had gotten too busy. I had chores to do and had to manage Sahir's office, and it only got busier as our family grew. Sabah stopped being the baby of the house. She had to step into the role of a big sister for her twin siblings. It was an unsaid understanding that she had to babysit while I worked. I had to fulfill my various responsibilities as secretary, office administrator, and interpreter.

I owe my comeback to Sabah. Cancer gave me absolute clarity of who my true family was. We had the love and support of a few parents at my children's school. They cooked for us and took turns taking my younger children home for sleepovers. They dropped them off at school the next day, all while I was dealing with my illness in the hospital. They are my angels.

Sahir and Maya decided to go on a vacation to Chicago during my period of struggle. Friends and neighbours came forward to give Sabah a hand and support us. They are my women tribe - the ones who make this world a beautiful place, the ones for whom there is still hope in humanity.

The teachers in the school empowered my children with support as well as with lunch on some days. My parents, siblings and new sister in law (brother's wife) indulged in prayers. My school friends organized global prayer chains. There were friends who remembered me during their travels and offered special prayers. Prayers were said worldwide in mosques, mausoleums, Buddhist temples and churches. My childhood friend prayed at the statue of Madonna. She stood in the freezing cold winter snow, before the crack of dawn to ask God to heal me. Love and prayers blanketed me. I am blessed and grateful for each one of them. No one from Sahir's family bothered to enquire about us. Not even those who would reach out to me to get some work done.

Notes:

Cancer was the Cure

I had "tremendous emotional agony and trauma trapped at a cellular level," said a healer from India. My sister happened to share with me about several healing modalities. That was the beginning of my spiritual journey. I was on a quest to heal. I did several courses in mindfulness and personal mastery. The more I explored myself in this journey of self-mastery, the hungrier I became. It was comforting, soothing, and therapeutic. Powerful healers showed up to heal me. I loved being in the space of no judgment and total self-acceptance. I discovered a whole world of people who were compassionate and selfless, without any agendas. I let go of many hand-me-down belief patterns and practiced whatever gave me peace. I broke barriers of religion and chose to see them as different expressions of the same concepts. I expanded in this openness.

My biggest breakthroughs came when I attended powerful leadership programs. I let go of the blaming, complaining and resentments. The shift happened when I chose to forgive not just others but myself too for the choices I made. That was a profound experience and I became more open-hearted. I took responsibility for whatever happened in my life.

I learned that we do not see things as *they* are. Instead, we tend to see them as *we* are. I discovered myself as a whole new being of love when I awakened to the idea that there was no wrong done and nothing to forgive. When I learned to take full responsibility for whatever happened in my life, I set myself free. I *agreed* to be free.

I had freed myself of my past and I was ready to design my tomorrow. Starting on a clean slate of a life in front of me and having a powerful context of living gave me super powers. I had rediscovered myself as a possibility of love, empowerment, and transformation. I became a stand for peoples' empowerment and fulfilled living. As I continued on this journey, the world became more magical for me. I began to create a future that is joyful and fantastic. I still have breakdowns, but I have acquired some skills to be present to my breakdowns and to deal with them powerfully. I reach out for guidance and ask for help from my tribe of elevated, loving, and nurturing beings.

I have spiritual guidance. To this day, I sit in meditation before the break of dawn. Meditation is what sustains and empowers me. I am spiritually guided and have pristine and powerful thoughts.

One of the secrets of my growth and expansion is humility. I begin each day in total surrender. I give up any thoughts of entitlement and create my world from nothing. In my experience, humility is, knowing my power and not taking it for granted. Humility allows me to be a learner for life and creates space for growth. It does not limit your expansion. Humility is the key to continuous self-mastery. Humility is the sacred recognition, and acceptance of the collaboration with the higher power - All That Is.

Knowledge began to flow to me as I showed readiness to receive it. Masters appeared as I showed willingness to learn. I continued working on myself to soften my being, and healing happened. In facing my fears of judgment, the more vulnerable and open I chose to be, the more I healed. To this day and speaking for the future, I continue to be work in progress; this is a lifetime process.

Cancer had cured me. It had done the heavy lifting for my spirit. I regained health from my illness. The scars on my throat are the only remnants.

A few years later, I was at an Asian restaurant for dinner with my children. As we were leaving, a Buddhist monk walked up to me. He said that he could see the light in my being and was curious to know what I did to have this light. I was humbled and grateful. This experience gave me some indication that I was on the right track!

I chose not to vanish into oblivion. I chose to spend my lonely nights in self-discovery and meditation. I chose to be a part of powerful communities. I continued to strive to be a healthy contribution to the world around me. I am now living purposefully and by my own design.

As a mother of three girls and a boy, I am present to my responsibilities as a parent. I am a stand for my girls that they may have a voice and they recognise the power of being women. I am a stand that my son does not grow up feeling privileged to be a man only by abusing the women in his life. We love each other as family members, and being a man or a woman does not change the way we love each other.

For a phase in my life, I went through tremendous hardship and suffering for being a woman. I forgive myself for choosing so much suffering and such a hard life. I did not have to make my life so hard. I am an educated girl who went to an institution that stands for women's empowerment. So, why did I compromise? I would stand up for anybody else going through the slightest of the sufferings I went through. What stopped me from standing for myself? In my human need to feel loved, why did I sacrifice my dignity and voice? Despite the education I had, why was I living my life in default?

The need for love made me do all that to myself. I was trying hard to live a life of validation. I was seeking approval and recognition from Sahir and his family. I realized that this was a never-ending story. My desperation for love and inclusion drove me to do things that were not at all in alignment with my being.

Notes: ✍

Happily Divorced

A friend from India once quoted, "it is better for a daughter to be dead than divorced". Her quote left me disturbed and concerned about her state of mind. The urgency to bring a shift to that kind of negative thinking was my aim. I am committed to removing the stigma that is attached to divorced women particularly in the South Asian community.

My home was broken from the legacy of hate that brewed between Sahir's sister's family and mine and the abusive culture of his family. The divorce created a breathing space for both of us. My family was more complete than ever after the divorce. There was no draining of energy in dealing with everyday ugliness. I had leaned back into love again and regained health and self-confidence. What is shameful and horrendous about any of these? I say that I am happily divorced.

As I continued to work on my spiritual self, I began to simplify and deconstruct every area of my life. Removing clutter also meant doing away with toxic relationships. If they were not a space for mutual love and growth, it was doing more harm than good.

My divorce was a relief from suffering, resentment, and ugly feelings that I experienced while being in a dysfunctional marriage, full of unreasonable expectations. Having cleared that, I am able to appreciate the moments with my kids.

My divorce was a release from the old pattern of subjugation enforced by cultural traditions- a way of life that no longer served me. People who were not contributing to me in a loving and respectful way had to be parted with.

My divorce stood for accepting and embracing everything that happened, and making peace with it. It involved the letting go of fear. The idea of letting go of fear was a fear in itself. I was afraid of being left alone to raise four young children single-handedly.

My divorce was my freedom to show up in the world as I am and be loved and accepted for the same. It was an opportunity to reset my life.

Yes, it took a divorce to recover and restore the dignity in the relationship between a man and a woman. Now that I am not his wife, I learned to set boundaries. Sometimes I wonder why is it easy for men to respect the women who are not in their family.

As I shared my life experiences, I learned that there was suffering for women everywhere. I learned that this was an epidemic on a global scale even in today's world that brags of so much progress. I met women from Mexico, Africa, Turkey, Lebanon, and

China and all of them had stories of abuse and suffering. Their suffering continued behind the closed doors of their homes, even in a progressive country like Canada.

I met a woman who was Canadian by birth and her great grandparents were Canadian too. She experienced physical abuse from a South Asian husband. "This was normally expected of men from South Asia", she said. When I questioned her silence, she justified his culture, so she accepted the injuries and scars as a part of the family cultural tradition of the South Asian man she was married to. She chose to compromise on her right to be treated right and with dignity, only to justify and hush it up and keep the marriage going.

There are more women like her and Maya everywhere. Women who choose to suffer and allow the men in their lives to feel privileged to abuse. They allow these men to strip a woman of her dignity of being human and her right to be treated equal in love and respect. Being a bystander and not taking a stand for oneself or for another is just as culpable as the abuser. Calling out a predator is a responsible act towards being a harbinger for change. I understand that it may jeopardize personal safety. What if we women put a structure in place to combat that?

Despite the fact that we are progressing, issues of addressing gender equality have suffered a setback. I appreciate the work that has been done so far. I have so much support if I choose to seek it. My question is why should we need to have to seek support and protection from one of my kind? What is not working between men and women? Why would a man love a woman only to pretend to honour the partnership? Why would he have children with her and yet not want to see her succeed and lead? Why is a successful and leading woman a threat to men? How does an abused woman make a man feel powerful? Do all women agree to be liberated and equal?

Before my second marriage, I was drifting through life like a severed kite. I was drifting aimlessly in the sky going with the flow of the wind and living a predictable life of mediocrity. Now I am putting this on the table with the intention of bringing a change. There has been enough suffering behind closed doors of homes. It is time to change the narrative of men abusing women and women abusing men. We were created as equal partners to empower and support each other. It is time to embrace the Divine in both the masculine and feminine. It is time to give up the polarity and discord to bring in balance and harmony.

Exercise:

- *It starts from you, yes you, who has read my story this far.*

- *I let you into my heart and ripped open my scars, wrote every word in the blood and tears of my sorrow.*

- *Will you be a game-changer in your family, at your workplace, with your friends?*

- *I invite you to choose to be the collective, the whole, and the complete.*

- *We are in this together.*

Notes: ✍

I am Not a Man and the World is Unfair

As a commitment to self-empowerment, I discovered that I had been living my whole life trapped in a perspective that "I am not a man and the world is unfair."

"You are my son, you are not my daughter." This was what I earned every time I showed up in my power. Why couldn't I be appreciated as a daughter? Why couldn't I be acknowledged as a very powerful and fulfilling dream *girl* child? Why did I have to be a *son* to receive that status and recognition?

"There can't be two men in the same house. You are a wife, and I am the man of the house. God is a He!" why would my leadership and success be a threat to someone who loves me? Is God really a masculine *he* or a neutral *He*? Does God have a human body to limit him to a specific gender?

Particularly in a traditional patriarchal family, a mother seeing her girl-child as an encumbrance creates the space for the father to only wish for a male child. Those women give men permission to abuse. They complain and demand dowry, destroy families and homes in their nastiness. When the women in the family do not have a voice, it allows several generations to get away with abuse. Abuse then takes on the guise of culture.

An example of this is leaving a will to empower the male descendants in the family only. This gesture ignores the female descendants. It discards their ability to be powerful leaders and role models in the family.

When a woman chooses to be a silent spectator to her man's cheating, it allows the man to abuse the rest of us. Before we speak of gender inequality, we need to show integrity and mutual respect for those of our kind.

Notes:

Giving Up Being Right, Choosing Love

In the past, I was functioning in survival mode. I was loaded with ammunitions of blaming others, self-pity, self-defence, and righteousness. My communications, thus, were more reactive than intentional. I was exhausted and stressed from this way of living. I was always trying very hard to convince and this would end up in arguments. We do what we do based on what we know and what we don't. That is the only truth.

As human beings we are doing our best. Our best is compromised by fears, interpretations, judgments, and ignorance. Hence there is this tendency to blame or defend ourselves or even self-sabotage our lives. Academic schools do not show us the way to deal with our own demons. When things go wrong in our lives, they do so to highlight what needs to change in our inner world. What thoughts, patterns, and beliefs do we need to let go of? How do we respond to crises in our lives? How do we handle adversity with grace and patience? How do we practice self-care during challenging times? How do we reset our lives? How do we ground ourselves and make a fresh start? Who do we seek advice from? How do we take responsibility for our lives, reinstate reliability and forgive ourselves? How do we practice self-love? How do we acknowledge and appreciate ourselves and others? How do we nurture gratitude within us for what we have? Why is it important to ask these questions?

Being on a journey of self-discovery and self-mastery is the biggest service we can offer to the people around us. The more we work on ourselves, the more we can be authentic and bring ease and openness in our interactions. After all *we hide nothing only when we have nothing to hide.*

Notes:

Be Your Own North Star

From the burnt embers of my being, the Phoenix of light was rising to shine. I was not the kind to wallow in the complacency of letting life go by. I was not done. Yes, I had so much to do in a day as a full-time single mother. Yet I had this compelling urge to be a stand for those who are invisible and suffering like I was.

I aspire for my children to live in a world of integrity, responsibility, and generosity. I yearn for others to become torchbearers of a new paradigm of possibilities.

I had not been through so much for nothing. What was the gold in my experiences? I had discovered my super power of resilience. This super power had come from my conviction to be unstoppable in the face of adversity. I am humbled by the experiences of love and empathy from people around the world. I have been healing in that love, quicker than what you can ever imagine. They say it takes a village to raise a child. I say it takes a whole world of loving people to restore a woman who went through abuse and suffering.

I had two choices in front of me. To choose the story of how a man hurt me or to choose the story of how a man gave me the opportunity to discover my own powers. I chose to experience profound lessons of life. I chose to make my story as a positive context for the future and a benchmark for building a deep sense of appreciation, sensitivity, and love. This further quickened the urgency to serve, and the *Shining Star Movement* was born. This movement encourages people to be their own guiding force while navigating through life. It is our inner GPS that we learn to access.

To *Be Your Own North Star* suggests choosing to live by your own inner wisdom and higher knowing. When we begin to rely on our own innate wisdom to navigate through life, we become our own North Stars. We find our own directions. We become powerful, self-aware and self-reliant.

We see the stars only in the darkness of night. It was my time to shine my light against the backdrop of the darkest phase of my life. The North Star or the Polaris is a guiding light, it is constant and unwavering. It gives directions to travellers. It helps us find our True North. Accurately finding the True North is important for navigators

Metaphorically, finding our True North in the journey of life enables us to follow the right direction. There are various ways of enabling a person and building human capacity. We could give someone money, impart education, or teach them a skill. But if they are not enabled with the tools of following their own inner guidance, they end up unfulfilled and suffering. Self-actualization allows us to expand and be resourceful for ourselves and for the world.

Notes: ✍

Summa cum Laude

I would say that I have done well in the lessons that my life had to teach me. I own my story with great humility. It was in my decision to get out of the comfort of my hiding, in making my way to the centre stage of my life that I discovered my true power.

I am a student of lifelong learning. I aspire to take my scholarship to the next level of excellence where my learning can serve others. I have shared my story with sincerity, openness and simplicity.

I have set the intention of creating a space of possibility, love, transformation and empowerment for those who are seeking to shift their lives. In this space, *you* are whole, perfect and complete just the way *you* are. In this space *you* have nothing to fear. In this space, *you* matter. In this space, *you* are no longer invisible and unheard. In this space, *you* belong. In this space, *I am* whole, perfect and complete just the way *I am*. In this space, *I* have nothing to fear. In this space, *I* matter. In this space, *I am* no longer invisible and unheard. In this space, *I* belong. This sacred space of no prejudice and no fragmentation, no separation unites us as one human race. Our pain and suffering is the cry of convergence for humankind to rise in rebellion to the clichéd ways of living.

I own my story and I am giving it away to *you*, choosing to create a conscious partnership with *you*. My story has no ending because *you* are my next chapter, my next book. My story continues. People around the world, especially women and children, are suffering. They are denied their basic rights.

When *you* share your own story, *you* then get to pass on the learning to another. It does not have to be perfect. *You* earn the privilege to serve another with the wisdom of your experiences. *You*, yes *you*, then get to break the status quo of a dysfunctional world. *You* then get to break the glass ceiling of global progress.

One story at a time, we are going to impact the world. Let us learn and grow and expand together so that no one is left behind. Every person on this planet has a story that could contribute to making a difference in the lives of others and leave a trail of goodness behind. Do you have a story that the world needs to hear?

Let us not hide anymore and be complacent to the suffering of another human being. Let us unlearn the old ways to create more freedom and ease. Let us be the harbingers of change. Let us hold our heads high in dignity and pride and create a movement in unison for all of humankind to participate. This world is as much yours as it is mine. We are only one human race and therefore always connected. Let us hold hands in building the capacity of this world together to do more and be more. Imagine what the whole world would bring to fruition if all the people loved one another. Let us collapse the notion of singularity and expand our vision to see ourselves as a collective, for abundance is the language of pluralism.

Notes:

A Love Note to Me

Small steps my love,
small steps each day.
A book here,
A speech there,
My heart has a say.

My dreams look so blurry,
The reason is new,
My eyes filled with tear drops
Like fresh morning dew
On a blade of green grass
In a lush meadow plain,
My spirit is humbled,
I want to be Shirin again!

Biography

Shirin was born in a very prestigious family of Kolkata. She was born of parents from diverse religious beliefs. And she was raised in an elite Catholic school run by Irish nuns (the Loreto Sisters). This diversity created the space for her to be open and receptive to people from different backgrounds.

She completed her Bachelor of Arts with a major in English and a Bachelor of Education from one of the finest institutions–Loreto College. She went on to teaching school children. Her most memorable experience as a teacher has been that of teaching the children of slum dwellers in a street school in India.

Her desire to be self-expressed found its way through writing. From a very young age Shirin wrote poetry that were published in the local newspaper.

Shirin's life has been quite a roller coaster ride. She overcame the challenges of two exhausting marriages that ended in relieving divorces. Moving to a new country and starting all over again as an immigrant with no family to support her was yet another challenge. Co-creating wealth in her husband's business and yet living financially compromised, experiencing Bell's palsy that paralyzed the right side of her face, delivering twins and overcoming metastasized Cancer, she has done it all!

Her comeback- She is more powerful than ever before. She is complete with her past. She is giving, nurturing, joyful and positive and lives her life in gratitude and humility.

Shirin stands tall as a single parent for her four beautiful and young children. She is a brave woman for nurturing herself back to health. People know her for her warm and friendly personality. She stands for love, grace, compassion, inspiration, transformation, empowerment and resilience.

Shirin shares her story and life experiences generously with others with the intention of empowering and transforming other women who are dealing with abuse and hardship and are invisible.

As part of her *Shining Star Movement*, Shirin has created a coaching program called *Be Your Own North Star* for women who are diminished and lost so that they can reset themselves to be their own guiding force.

You can reach Shirin here:
www.beyourownnorthstar.com

Notes: ✎

www.ingramcontent.com/pod-product-compliance
Lightning Source LLC
Chambersburg PA
CBHW072249270326
41930CB00010B/2319